WILLIAMS-SONOMA

Easy
ENTERTAINING

RECIPES AND FOOD STYLING

George Dolese

GENERAL EDITOR

Chuck Williams

PHOTOGRAPHY

Anna Williams

STYLING

Robin Turk

TEXT

Steve Siegelman

NEW YORK · LONDON · TORONTO · SYDNEY

CONTENTS

MORNING

AFTERNOON

EVENING

the art of easy entertaining

Some of the most memorable meals I have enjoyed with friends—whether as host or guest—have been impromptu get-togethers. A lobster dinner served on mismatched plates at a beach house. An after-movie supper with big bowls of pasta improvised from whatever was in the refrigerator. An alfresco meal of antipasti and salads picked up at the last minute from a local deli.

What all these meals have in common is a relaxed yet vibrant mood—and what they celebrate is friendship. There is no thought of impressing guests with fancy food or of fussing over elaborate decorations. The dishes and drinks satisfy without stealing the show. The guests feel as if they are "family," the host gets to join the party, and laughter and lively conversation flow naturally as the hours slip by. If only all entertaining could be so stress free.

The truth is, it can. And in today's complicated world, it should be. It seems a shame to spend too much time in the kitchen away from your friends and the fun. Of course, entertaining cannot always be a spur-of-the-moment affair, but you can approach any entertaining occasion, even a dinner party planned weeks in advance, with that same spirit of informality, spontaneity, and casual ease. This book will show you how to do just that.

You'll find failproof menus, recipes, decorating ideas, and tips, all designed for the way busy people live and cook today. First-rate prepared foods and ingredients that free you to spend less time in the kitchen are more readily available than ever before, even at your local supermarket. By taking advantage of these items—adding simple touches to make them your own—you will discover that entertaining really can be effortless. And the more relaxed you are, the more fun everyone will have.

Chuck Williams

keeping it simple

Why don't people entertain more often? Time, stress, work, cooking ability, and limited space are common reasons. Forget them all. Entertaining is about sharing good food and drink with friends and family, and whether you are hosting a casual breakfast or an elegant dinner party, the experience can be fun and easy. All it takes is planning, a few trustworthy recipes and serving ideas, and smart shopping.

your space will work

Once you've settled on the occasion—be it a birthday, a holiday, or just a chance to bring together a group of friends—think creatively about where to entertain. A meal doesn't have to mean a dining-room table. Picture your guests enjoying themselves around a kitchen island, on the patio, in the backyard, in front of the fireplace, or even at a local park or beach. Choose a location that feels appropriate, and think about how to make the space work. Your guests are not looking to be impressed. They want to spend a few pleasurable hours together. Let ease and comfort be your guiding principles.

setting on a style

Now, think about how you will serve the meal. Of course, you want to entertain with flair. But remember, simplicity is a style, and no matter how many people you are inviting or how formal the occasion, it is a style that never fails. Simple doesn't need to mean minimalist or boring. It can be exciting, abundant, and festive. The secret is to keep the food and the way you serve it uncomplicated. A bare wood table or a crisply ironed linen tablecloth; flowers fresh from the garden; plates, glasses, and platters with clean lines—these are the kinds of elements that make any table welcoming.

For groups of eight or more, buffets are your best choice. Pull a table away from the wall to allow easy access from both sides, then set out platters and serving utensils to see how everything fits. Plan to arrange the food in the order in which it will be eaten. The more you think everything through ahead of time, the less you will have to worry about at the last minute. For smaller groups, serve food family style from passed platters and bowls. This type of service can be as homey or refined as you like, depending on the platters and other serving ware you choose and the way you arrange the food on them.

Serving restaurant style, with each guest's plate composed in the kitchen, is a nice approach, but it is not always the easiest, requiring more last-minute work for the cook. Consider making a first course that is easily served in single portions, such as a creamed soup, for added refinement with minimal extra work. Then serve the main course and side dishes family style.

strategic shopping

Today's grocery stores and specialty-food shops offer more time-saving ingredients and company-worthy prepared foods than ever. The best way to master the art of easy entertaining is to start by surveying these options at stores near your home or office. A supermarket with a good deli, a farmers' market, a wine shop, and a bakery are probably all you will need.

shopping tips

As you shop, get in the habit of making mental notes of products that can save you time—vacuum-packed precooked beets, cut-up fruits, prewashed greens, shaved Parmesan cheese, grilled vegetables from the deli, peeled and deveined shrimp from the seafood counter. These products are the simple secret to many of the recipes in this book. They will cut out recipe steps and prep time without compromising flavor and finished appearance.

Good butchers and fishmongers are also wonderful resources. Place your order in advance so it's ready when you arrive, and ask for the items to be prepared as fully as possible—fish filleted; meats trimmed, tied, or sliced; oysters shucked, packed on ice, and ready to serve.

Try to remember that guests don't expect you to make everything yourself. Good food is good food. Purchasing one or more courses can make a huge difference in the amount of time it takes to put together a meal. Look for fully prepared items such as stuffed olives, cubes of marinated feta, seasoned bread sticks, cured meats sliced paper-thin, home-style pies or tarts, or fancy chocolates, cookies, and pastries. Every week when you shop, pick up something new to try, so that you gradually build a "library" of options that will work for entertaining. Serve them just as they are, arranged on plates, adding a little touch to personalize them if you wish—a fresh herb sprig, a splash of extra-virgin olive oil, a sprinkle of shredded cheese, a dollop of whipped cream, a handful of fresh berries.

the food

The greatest gift you can give yourself when hosting a party is to avoid the urge to be too ambitious. As you plan your menu, start simple and build from there, with an eye toward foods that can be prepared or assembled ahead of time and served with minimal last-minute attention. Use the meals and ideas in this book as a guide. Keep in mind what is realistic for the occasion, the setting, the number of guests, and your level of skill. Don't forget some store-bought salty snacks to serve with drinks when your guests first arrive

Choose foods that fit the season and the weather. Fresh produce, prepared with a light hand, is ideal for easy entertaining any time of year. Dishes like crisp salad greens drizzled with vinaigrette and accompanied with a slice of cheese, colorful fruit skewers, or roasted asparagus can be just as pleasing, attractive, and flavorful as more elaborate and time-consuming preparations. Balance your choices with some meatless options for guests who prefer a lighter meal. And always plan a menu that offers a variety of colors, textures, and flavors.

easy appetizers

Setting out a variety of savory tidbits ahead of time is a great idea—your guests will have something to nibble on with drinks as soon as they arrive. Remember to allow chilled items to come to room temperature for the best flavor. Don't forget a small dish for olive pits and nut shells. The following quick-to-assemble appetizers use store-bought items.

Marcona Almonds Look for these Spanish blanched almonds, sold roasted with oil and salt, at specialty-food markets; toss with coarsely chopped rosemary leaves and/or red pepper flakes.

Bocconcini Skewer these bite-sized balls of fresh mozzarella with cherry tomatoes and fresh basil leaves on decorative picks.

Edamame These fresh soybeans, cooked in the pod, are sold in the freezer section of most supermarkets; boil and serve with salt.

Crostini Spread thin toasted baguette rounds with store-bought tapenade or onion jam, or layer with fresh ricotta or goat cheese, prosciutto, and sliced fig.

"Doctored" Olives Dress up jarred olives or a mix of favorites from a good olive bar by tossing them with olive oil, minced herbs, and lemon or orange zest.

Cured Meats Buy thinly sliced Italian cured meats, such as coppa and salami. Plan on about one ounce (30 g) total per guest. Roll each slice and arrange the slices on a platter; serve with crackers or bread sticks.

Meze Platter Set out bowls of hummus, baba ghanoush, stuffed grape leaves, and olives. Cut a stack of pita bread into wedges and serve alongside in a napkin-lined basket.

the drinks

Setting up a bar or beverage tray in advance will make any party run more smoothly—even an intimate gathering. This can be as straightforward as putting beverages, ice, glassware, and cocktail napkins in a designated spot. Rather than taking drink orders, greet guests with a tray of already-prepared cocktails or flutes filled with sparkling wine as a welcoming way to begin. If you plan to serve a drink made with alcohol, prepare a nonalcoholic option as well. For large groups, consider buying bagged ice instead of relying on the trays in your freezer; figure on 1 to 1½ pounds (500 to 750 g) of ice per person.

Once you have your menu in mind, call your local wine store and ask the merchant for recommendations. Place the order ahead of time and request that it be ready for pick up at the register. Or, even easier, buy your favorite everyday red and white wines and sparkling water by the case, so you're always ready for company.

general supplies

Outfit yourself with a few well-chosen basics and keep them together for quick access:

- Serving platters, trays, boards, pitchers, and carafes
- Small dishes for olives, nuts, and dips; cheese board, knives, and spreaders
- Candles (votives, pillars, and tapers), vases, and place cards
- Wine cooler, ice bucket, corkscrew, coasters, and cocktail napkins
- Music (make your own playlists or CDs)

the pantry

For "instant entertaining," stock up with your favorite packaged items:

- Nuts (almonds, cashews, and pistachios)
- Crackers, bread sticks, and gourmet chips
- Jars of olives, marinated artichoke hearts, and marinated feta cheese
- Red or green salsa
- Sun-dried tomatoes marinated in olive oil
- Stuffed cherry peppers
- Olive tapenade or truffle spread

serving beverages

For planning purposes, allow one bottle of wine and one quart (1 l) of water for every two or three guests. For a sit-down dinner, wait until the guests are seated before pouring the wine. Fill glasses one-third full. Serving wines at the proper temperature brings out their best qualities. Sparkling wines should be very well chilled and stored in an ice bucket. You can offer them as an aperitif, with the first course, or serve them throughout the meal. Chill white wines in the refrigerator, and serve reds and most dessert wines at cool room temperature. Remember to have plenty of nonalcoholic options on hand. Offer chilled still or sparkling water throughout the meal—lemon slices, mint sprigs, or cucumber disks add a refreshing hit of flavorful color to water. After dinner, offer espresso or coffee, tea (including an herbal option, such as peppermint or chamomile), and perhaps a dessert wine.

the setting

Take care of all the basic supplies and you'll be ready to entertain any time, whether it's a long-planned dinner party or a spur-of-the-moment meal shared with unexpected guests. Here is a simple starter plan for the serving and decorative elements you need to set a welcoming table. Master it, and you won't have to begin anew every time you invite people to your house.

the setting

When it comes to decorating, a little advance planning will be time well spent. Here again, less is usually more. You may even want to begin by clearing away some items from the party space, so you can create a unified look. For a casual meal, consider a runner or place mats instead of a tablecloth. When in doubt, stick with white or off-white and one or two accent colors.

Repeated visual patterns are relaxing and pleasing to the eye. Set napkins, rolled or folded, at each plate. For an extra touch, add a small wrapped gift or a single flower to each setting. For larger sit-down dinners, include decorative place cards. Use natural elements to create unfussy centerpieces and decorations, such as a bowl filled with lemons or limes or an assortment of glass bottles with fresh-cut flowers. Pillar candles or votives in colored or faceted glasses are an easy way to add sparkle. Music also helps to set the mood; pick out some favorite tracks before the guests arrive.

setting the mood

Decorative Elements: Limit decorations to a handful of beautiful elements in only a few colors. They can be elegant or earthy, antique or modern. If you want to create a centerpiece, keep it low, so that it won't block sight lines at the table. Anything from a crystal vase to old-fashioned glass bottles filled with flowers will work—just keep the overall look focused, clean, and harmonious. Natural, seasonal elements, such as fruits, leaves, and garden flowers, are a pleasing, inexpensive choice for a casual centerpiece. You can also use them directly on the tabletop, as accents at each place setting, and to decorate the buffet, the bar, and any other surfaces.

Lighting: Dim overhead lights and use lamps and candles to create an intimate mood. Votives in glass containers or pillar candles, lined up along the center of the table or around the centerpiece, both work well. If you use tapers, choose tall ones, so that the flame remains above eye level when guests are seated at the table. Use the same kind of candles on the buffet to tie the room together. White or off-white candles will go with any setting.

the table

A comfortable table setting should allow about two feet (60 cm) of space between the center of one plate and the center of the next. Add leaves or extensions as needed.

Dishes: Basic white dinner plates are ideal for any kind of occasion and menu. You can supplement them with patterned or colored serving dishes to create a classic or modern look. Use matching plates for each course if you have them, but don't worry about uniformity from course to course. Count out your dishes in advance and buy or borrow more if you don't have enough.

Flatware: A set of plain, nicely weighted, silver-toned flatware will work for any type of meal. Rather than using kitchen spoons for serving, you might want to invest in some vintage or modern pieces, such as large spoons, serving forks, and a cake server. Set out your serving utensils ahead of time, so you don't have to search for them at the last minute.

Glassware: Two simple sets of glasses—wineglasses and tumblers—are all you need for easy entertaining. All-purpose white-wine glasses are a good starter choice because they can also be used for red wine. Even an inexpensive set can bring a tabletop together by adding sparkle, and their matching shapes and sizes create a pleasing pattern.

Linens: For casual entertaining, a simple, understated cotton or linen tablecloth in a neutral color is a versatile choice; or, if you have an attractive table, consider using place mats, or set cool dishes directly on the table surface. Cloth napkins, even simple ones, are an easy way to make every occasion feel more special and add a touch of color. They don't need to match the tablecloth, but they should complement its color and style. You can add interest to each place setting by tying or folding the napkin

in a creative way and incorporating a decorative element, such as a small gift, a name tag, or a fresh-cut flower or spray of foliage that matches the centerpiece.

the details

Once the food and the table are ready, carefully review the final details. Take care of any outstanding chores, like emptying the dishwasher and the kitchen trash can and sweeping the kitchen floor. Don't forget to designate an area where guests can put their coats as they arrive. Make sure the bathroom is stocked with fresh towels, soap, and perhaps a vase of flowers or a candle. Set out the linens, glassware, dishes, platters, and serving utensils you will need. Chill any beverages you will be serving, adjust the lighting, and ready the music you plan to play. Write out the menu along with a timetable for cooking, assembling, and serving and post them in the kitchen. Check off each task as you complete it.

easy does it

A good host keeps everyone happy without anyone noticing. And the key to being that kind of host is to keep things uncomplicated and organized for yourself. Do as much as you can ahead of time, and let prepared foods and quality ingredients take you the rest of the way. Remember, your attitude is important: If you're relaxed and having fun, your guests will be, too. Don't worry about trying to impress anyone—keep in mind your guests simply want to spend a few joyful hours with you sharing a meal. Use the menus and ideas in this book for inspiration, mixing and matching, if you like, to find what works best for you. Use the style ideas and serving suggestions as a starting point for your own creativity, drawing on what's available around you and in season for inspiration. You'll discover that no matter what you make or how you serve it, if you make the process easy, you can turn entertaining into one of life's joys.

morning

casual breakfast

tips and shopping notes

- A bunch of flowers of a single type, such as tulips or garden roses, in a clear glass vase is all the decoration you need.

- Slice chilled unsalted butter into pats and arrange on a pretty plate. Cover with plastic wrap and refrigerate until needed.

- Put lumps of white and brown sugar in a small, plain dish for a more interesting look than a traditional sugar bowl.

- The day before, pick up a loaf of brioche or crusty artisanal bread at a bakery on your way home from work.

- Measure ground coffee and set up the pot before guests arrive. Set out a teapot and a selection of tea bags at the same time.

menu

Melon Cider Fizz

•

Fruit Skewers

•

*Baked Egg Ramekins with
Ham, Brie, and Chives*

•

Toasted Brioche

work plan

IN ADVANCE

Thread the fruits on skewers

Assemble the egg ramekins

JUST BEFORE SERVING

Mix the melon drinks

Arrange the fruit skewers on a garnished platter

Toast the brioche

Bake the egg ramekins

melon cider fizz

5 MINUTES
PREPARATION

GARNISHING TIP
Thread each
melon ball onto
a bamboo skewer
that guests can use
to stir their drinks.

Italian-style flavored syrups are available at most grocery stores. For a colorful variation, try apricot, watermelon, orange, or raspberry syrup. On special occasions, use Prosecco, cava, or California sparkling wine instead of the cider.

Put 4 Champagne flutes or wineglasses in the freezer to chill for at least 15 minutes. Pour 2 tablespoons of the melon syrup into each chilled flute. Slowly fill the flutes with the sparkling cider, and then garnish each glass with a melon ball.

SERVES 4

1/2 cup (4 fl oz/125 ml) melon-flavored syrup

1 bottle (24 fl oz/750 ml) sparkling pear cider, well chilled

4 honeydew melon balls or cubes

fruit skewers

10 MINUTES
PREPARATION

SHOPPING TIP
Look for strawberries
with bright green
leaves and a shiny
color. Pass up berries
with green or
white shoulders.

Save time by buying precut fresh fruit in plastic containers. You can make this refreshing treat with any seasonal combination, including honeydew melon, watermelon, large seedless grapes, and papaya. Leftover fruit pieces can be frozen in a zippered plastic bag to use in smoothies or other blended fruit drinks.

Have ready 12 small bamboo skewers. Thread the cantaloupe, pineapple, and strawberries onto the skewers, arranging them in a decorative pattern and dividing them evenly. (The fruit skewers can be prepared up to this point, covered with plastic wrap, and refrigerated for up to 2 hours.)

To serve, make a bed of the mint sprigs on a serving platter. Arrange the fruit skewers on top. Serve at once.

SERVES 4

1 container (8 oz/250 g) fresh cantaloupe pieces

1 container (8 oz/250 g) fresh pineapple pieces

2 baskets (8 oz/250 g each) strawberries, hulls removed

1 bunch fresh mint

baked egg ramekins with ham, brie, and chives

4 tablespoons (2 oz/60 g) unsalted butter

8 large eggs

2 slices ham, 3 oz (90 g) total weight, cut into narrow strips

$^1/_4$ lb (125 g) Brie cheese, end rind removed, cut into small cubes

2 tablespoons chopped fresh chives

Coarse salt and freshly ground pepper

Toasted brioche slices (see tip)

For a vegetarian version, substitute 1 cup (3 oz/90 g) sautéed mushrooms for the ham. Other soft cheeses, such as Camembert or a creamy fresh goat cheese, will work in place of the Brie. For added ease, assemble the ramekins the night before, cover with plastic wrap, and refrigerate until ready to bake.

Preheat the oven to 375°F (190°C). Bring a tea kettle filled with water to a boil. Place four ¾-cup (6–fl oz/180-ml) ramekins in a deep baking pan.

Place 1 tablespoon of the butter in each ramekin. Carefully break 2 eggs into each ramekin. Scatter the ham strips and Brie cubes evenly over the eggs. Sprinkle with the chives and season with salt and pepper.

Pour boiling water into the baking pan until it reaches halfway up the sides of the ramekins. Cover the pan with aluminum foil and bake until the egg whites are firm and the yolks are still soft, 10–12 minutes.

Remove the pan from the oven and carefully remove the ramekins from the water bath. Place each ramekin on an individual plate with a couple of brioche slices on the side. Serve at once.

SERVES 4

10 MINUTES PREPARATION

12 MINUTES COOKING

COOKING TIP
Buy a brioche loaf or individual brioches at a bakery a day ahead. Slice or split and arrange on a baking sheet before the guests arrive. Toast the slices in the broiler, leaving the door ajar and checking every few minutes to avoid burning.

brunch buffet

tips and shopping notes

- For an informal buffet, arrange platters on the kitchen counter or kitchen table to allow guests to serve themselves.

- Put the silverware in a deep bowl with the handles pointing out for easy access.

- A tray of bubbly drinks made with fruit juice, such as peach nectar spritzers or mimosas (sparkling wine and orange juice), passed as the guests arrive, is a festive way to begin.

- Fill decanters with ice water and store-bought fresh-squeezed orange juice and place on or near the buffet. You can also set out insulated pitchers of coffee and tea.

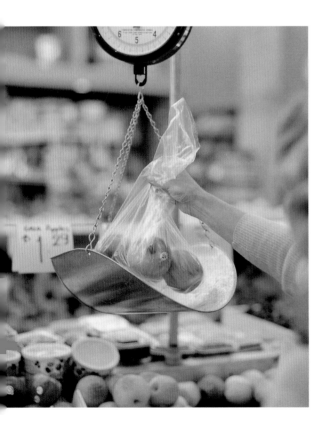

menu

Peach Nectar Spritzers

·

Smoked Salmon
with a Selection of Garnishes

·

Herbed Cream Cheese

·

Potato and Beet Salad with Dill

·

Apple Cake

work plan

IN ADVANCE

Assemble the salmon platter

Mix the cream cheese spread

Prepare the potato and beet salad

Bake the cake

JUST BEFORE SERVING

Place the garnishes in bowls

Mix the spritzers

select an attractive, sturdy tray. A simple wooden tray looks particularly nice with natural decorations, such as fresh foliage.

snip blossoms, leaves, and small branches from a bush or tree in your garden, or buy blooms from a florist.

arrange the unfilled glasses on the tray, spacing them generously. Just before the guests arrive, tuck the flowers around the glasses, keeping them low and out of the way.

peach nectar spritzers

Fruit nectar adds a splash of color and flavor to a glass of refreshing sparkling water. Use the nectar of a fruit that is in season so that you can garnish each drink with a few slices of the same fruit.

Ice cubes

2 cans (12 fl oz/375 ml each) peach nectar

1 bottle (24 fl oz/750 ml) sparkling mineral water

1 peach, halved, pitted, and thinly sliced

Fill 6 tall glasses half full with ice cubes. Pour ½ cup (4 fl oz/125 ml) of the peach nectar into each glass and fill with the sparkling water. (Alternatively, fill a pitcher half full with ice cubes, pour both cans of peach nectar into the pitcher, and stir in the sparkling water.)

Garnish each glass with a few peach slices. Serve at once.

SERVES 6

5 MINUTES PREPARATION

smoked salmon with a selection of garnishes

15 MINUTES
PREPARATION

SHOPPING TIP
Sprouts are sold in
bunches or clear
plastic boxes. Look
for slender sprouts
that smell clean
and are crisp and
moist. Refrigerate
the sprouts in
the container or
loosely packed in
a plastic bag.

Once considered a hard-to-find delicacy, sliced smoked salmon is now available at most markets. It is sold in a variety of types, from simply smoked to rubbed with herbs. To add visual interest, serve at least two different types.

Separate the slices of smoked salmon. Working with 1 slice at a time, cut or break into small pieces and transfer to a chilled serving platter. Repeat with the remaining slices. (The salmon can be prepared up to this point, covered with plastic wrap, and refrigerated for up to 24 hours.)

To serve, place each garnish in a small bowl and arrange on the salmon platter. Accompany with a basket of sliced breads.

SERVES 6

1¹/₂ lb (750 g) assorted sliced smoked salmon

Assorted garnishes such as rinsed capers, cucumbers, onion sprouts, radish sprouts, sweet mustard, pickled red onions, chopped chives, sliced tomatoes, or sprigs of watercress

Herbed Cream Cheese (below)

Assorted thinly sliced artisanal breads such as rye, pumpernickel, Nordic brown bread, whole-wheat (wholemeal) baguette, and dark walnut bread

herbed cream cheese

5 MINUTES
PREPARATION

SERVING TIP
Set up a tray ahead
of time with extra
accompaniments for
the salmon platter.
Keep it in the
refrigerator so
that you can quickly
replenish the buffet
as needed.

Whipped cream cheese is the starting point for this quick spread to accompany the smoked salmon platter. It is also a great condiment for baked potatoes, roasted beef, or poached salmon. You can substitute fresh dill, basil, or chervil for one or both of the herbs.

In a food processor, combine the cream cheese, sour cream, horseradish, chives, tarragon, and peppercorns. Pulse until the herbs and peppercorns are well distributed throughout the cream cheese.

Using a rubber spatula, scrape out the cream cheese into a small serving bowl. Cover with plastic wrap and store in the refrigerator for up to 24 hours. Serve chilled.

SERVES 6

1 container (8 oz/250 g) whipped cream cheese

¹/₂ cup (4 oz/125 g) sour cream

2 tablespoons creamy-style prepared horseradish

1 tablespoon chopped fresh chives

1 tablespoon chopped fresh tarragon

1 teaspoon drained brined green peppercorns

potato and beet salad with dill

DRESSING

1/2 cup (4 oz/125 g) sour cream

1 tablespoon mayonnaise

1 teaspoon creamy-style prepared horseradish

2 tablespoons chopped fresh dill

Salt and freshly ground pepper

2 packages (16 oz/500 g each) precooked "pearl" potatoes

1 package (8 oz/250 g) ready-to-eat beets, cut into small cubes

Chopped fresh dill for garnish

Steamed, peeled, and vacuum-packed beets and potatoes are ready to eat, making them ideal for this no-fuss salad. The beets are also wonderful as a plated first course, sliced and served with crumbled goat cheese, toasted walnuts, and your favorite vinaigrette.

To make the dressing, in a large bowl, combine the sour cream, mayonnaise, horseradish, and dill. Season to taste with salt and pepper.

Fold the potatoes and beets into the dressing.

Cover the bowl with plastic wrap and place in the refrigerator for at least 30 minutes or up to 24 hours to allow the flavors to blend. When ready to serve, transfer the potato salad to a serving bowl and garnish with dill.

SERVES 6

10 MINUTES PREPARATION

30 MINUTES RESTING

MAKE-AHEAD TIP
This salad can be made up to 24 hours in advance. Cover with plastic wrap and refrigerate until ready to serve.

apple cake

15 MINUTES
PREPARATION

60 MINUTES
COOKING

PREPARATION TIP
To prevent the
apple slices from
darkening while
you assemble
the other cake
ingredients, toss
the slices with the
juice of 1 lemon.

Buying nuts that are already finely ground will reduce the prep and cleanup time for any recipe that calls for ground nuts. Store the nuts in an airtight container in the freezer for several months.

Preheat the oven to 350°F (180°C). Generously butter a 9-inch (23-cm) nonstick springform pan.

In a bowl, using an electric mixer on medium-high speed, beat together the butter, granulated sugar, and salt until creamy. Add the eggs one at a time, beating well after each addition, and continue to beat until light and fluffy. Using a rubber spatula, fold in the ground nuts and baking powder. Add the apple slices to the batter, stirring until they are evenly coated. Pour the mixture into the prepared springform pan, spreading it in an even layer. If desired, use a fork to arrange the top layer of apple slices in a decorative pattern.

Bake until the top is golden and a toothpick inserted into the center of the cake comes out clean, 55–60 minutes. Let the apple cake cool in the pan on a wire rack for 30 minutes before serving.

To serve, release the sides of the pan and lift off the ring. Carefully slide a thin metal spatula under the cake to loosen it from the bottom of the pan. Using the spatula for support, slide the cake onto a serving platter. Serve the cake warm or at room temperature. (The cake can be prepared up to this point, covered with plastic wrap, and kept at room temperature for up to 24 hours.)

Just before serving, use a fine-mesh sieve to dust the top with confectioners' sugar, then cut the cake into wedges. Serve the cake at room temperature.

SERVES 6

1/2 cup (4 oz/125 g) unsalted butter, at room temperature

1/2 cup (4 oz/125 g) granulated sugar

1/2 teaspoon salt

3 large eggs

1 cup (4 oz/125 g) finely ground nuts such as almonds, walnuts, or hazelnuts (filberts)

1 teaspoon baking powder

6 apples such as Gala or Rome Beauty, peeled, cored, and thinly sliced

Confectioners' (icing) sugar for dusting

afternoon

elegant lunch

work plan

IN ADVANCE

Make the soup

Assemble the dessert plate

Prepare the salad dressing

JUST BEFORE SERVING

Mix the kir

Make the chicken salad

Reheat the soup

tips and shopping notes

- Passing drinks on a gleaming silver tray elevates the simple wine cocktail and sets a festive mood.

- Casual bouquets of pastel flowers such as lilacs or hydrangeas serve as centerpieces.

- Set the table with a neatly pressed linen or cotton tablecloth.

- Use crystal or glass vases, bowls, and stemware with silver accent pieces for sparkling elegance.

- For wine, serve a light-bodied Pinot Noir for a red and a dry Sauvignon Blanc (also known as Fumé Blanc) for a white.

Passionfruit
$1.25

menu

Blackberry Kir

•

Creamed Broccoli Leek Soup

•

Shredded Chicken Salad with
Sherry Dressing

•

Composed Dessert Plate

blackberry kir

5 MINUTES
PREPARATION

Kir, the classic French aperitif, is traditionally made by adding a splash of crème de cassis to a glass of chilled dry white wine. Rich blackberry liqueur brings a new twist and distinctive flavor dimension to this popular—and effortless—wine cocktail.

SERVING TIP
To make a drink with a lower alcohol content, use a blackberry-flavored syrup in place of the liqueur.

Put 4 wineglasses in the freezer to chill for at least 15 minutes.

Pour 1 tablespoon of the blackberry liqueur into each chilled glass. Fill the glasses two-thirds full with the wine. Serve at once.

SERVES 4

¼ cup (2 fl oz/60 ml) blackberry liqueur

1 bottle (24 fl oz/750 ml) Sauvignon Blanc or Chablis, well chilled

creamed broccoli leek soup

3 tablespoons olive oil

2 cloves garlic

1 package (12 oz/375 g) precut broccoli crowns or florets

1 leek, including tender, pale green part, finely chopped

1 tablespoon coarse-grain mustard

2 tablespoons fresh oregano leaves, plus a few leaves for garnish

4 cups (32 fl oz/1 l) vegetable or low-sodium chicken broth

1/4 cup (2 fl oz/60 ml) heavy (double) cream

Coarse salt and freshly ground pepper

Crumbled blue cheese for garnish

To make this smooth and creamy soup, look for all-natural, full-flavored vegetable or chicken broth sold in 1-quart (1-l) cartons. For a tangier flavor, use a crumbled goat cheese in place of the blue cheese garnish.

In a large saucepan over medium-high heat, warm the olive oil. Add the garlic, broccoli, leek, and mustard and sauté until the leek is soft and translucent and the broccoli is bright green, about 5 minutes. Add the oregano and broth and bring to a boil. Reduce the heat to low, cover partially, and simmer until the broccoli is tender, about 20 minutes.

Remove from the heat and process with an immersion blender or food processor until smooth. Stir in the cream and season to taste with salt and pepper. (The soup can be prepared up to this point, cooled, covered, and refrigerated for up to 24 hours. When ready to serve, reheat gently over medium-low heat, thinning the soup with more broth if needed.)

Ladle into warmed bowls and top each serving with a little blue cheese and a sprinkle of oregano leaves. Serve at once.

SERVES 4

15 MINUTES PREPARATION

25 MINUTES COOKING

SHOPPING TIP
Buy precut broccoli crowns or florets to minimize prep time in the kitchen.

shredded chicken salad with sherry dressing

15 MINUTES
PREPARATION

30 SECONDS
COOKING

SHOPPING TIP
Buy a good-quality
rotisserie chicken a
day ahead of time and
store it, well wrapped,
in the refrigerator.

Rotisserie chickens are versatile time-savers that can now be found at many supermarkets. Here, you shred the chicken meat for a salad, but you can also shred or dice it for use in other dishes good for entertaining, such as soups, pastas, enchiladas, or sandwiches. Or, you can carve the chicken for an easy main course.

To make the dressing, in a food processor, combine the mayonnaise, sour cream, sherry, soy sauce, and green onions. Purée until smooth and emulsified. Season to taste with salt and pepper. Transfer to a small bowl, cover, and refrigerate until ready to serve. (The dressing can be prepared in advance and refrigerated for up to 24 hours.)

Bring a small saucepan half full of water to a boil, add the peas, and blanch for 30 seconds. Drain the peas and refresh them under running cold water. Set aside to let drain completely.

Remove the skin from the roasted chicken and discard. Using your fingers, pull the meat from the bones and shred it into bite-sized pieces.

In a large bowl, combine the chicken meat, celery, watercress, walnut pieces, and peas. Add the dressing and toss to coat the salad evenly. To serve, divide the salad among chilled individual plates. Serve at once.

SERVES 4

DRESSING

1/2 cup (4 fl oz/125 ml) mayonnaise

1/4 cup (2 oz/60 g) sour cream

3 tablespoons dry sherry

1 tablespoon soy sauce

2 green (spring) onions, including tender green tops, chopped

Coarse salt and freshly ground pepper

1 cup (5 oz/155 g) frozen petite peas

1 roasted chicken, about 4 lb (2 kg)

1 celery stalk, thinly sliced

1 bunch young, tender watercress, tough stems removed

1/3 cup (1 1/2 oz/45 g) walnut pieces

gather pretty footed glass and silver serving platters and bowls in a variety of sizes and heights. Group them together on the table to make a pleasing arrangement.

purchase a selection of bakery cookies, premium chocolates, and fruit gelées, allowing 3 or 4 pieces total per person. Look for small sizes and delicate colors.

garnish each plate or bowl with a sprig of fresh mint. Serve chocolates in their paper cups, making them easy to pick up and eat.

composed dessert plate

When buying your selection of premium chocolates, three different varieties are plenty, such as liqueur filled, truffle filled, and caramel or nut filled. Pick out French-style macaroons, bite-sized tea wafers, or other small specialty cookies for your presentation. Or, use cream-filled petits fours in place of the cookies. Round out the offerings with fruit gelées, which deliver a hint of color and fresh flavor. Accompany with tea and/or coffee.

12 cookies

12 chocolates

12 fruit gelées

Fill attractive serving plates and bowls with an array of cookies, chocolates, and fruit gelées and place in the center of the table.

To serve, provide small plates for guests to assemble their own selection. For more casual dessert service, encourage guests to nibble directly from the serving plates, relaxing and conversing while sampling the various choices.

SERVES 4

5 MINUTES PREPARATION

backyard bbq

tips and shopping notes

- Set the food and drinks on tables near the kitchen, so they can be easily replenished.

- Fill a galvanized bucket with ice and a selection of assorted beers, bottled waters, and sodas.

- Provide extra napkins or sheets of waxed paper for guests to wrap their sandwiches, to guard against drips.

- Purchase two ready-made pies, tarts, or galettes for dessert; serve with ice cream.

- For wine, serve a fruity, spicy Zinfandel for a red and a medium-dry Riesling for a white.

menu

Vanilla Lemon Coolers

·

Grilled Sausages, Portobello Mushrooms,
and Onions

·

Pasta Salad with Grilled Vegetables

·

Cherry Tomato, Parmesan,
and Arugula Salad

·

Seasonal Fruit Pies with Ice Cream

work plan

IN ADVANCE

Mix the lemon coolers

Assemble the pasta salad

JUST BEFORE SERVING

Grill the sausages, mushrooms, and onions

Make the arugula salad

Dress the pasta salad

Cut the pies and accompany with ice cream

vanilla lemon coolers

Aromatic pure vanilla paste is sold in jars alongside vanilla extract (essence). It can be used to flavor both hot and cold beverages, including black tea, coffee, hot chocolate, apple juice, and, as shown here, lemonade.

4 qt (4 l) prepared lemonade
2 tablespoons vanilla paste
1 vanilla bean, split in half lengthwise
1 lemon, thinly sliced
Ice cubes for serving

Pour the lemonade into 2 large glass pitchers, dividing it evenly. Add 1 tablespoon of the vanilla paste to each pitcher and stir until dissolved. Place one-half of the vanilla bean in each pitcher, cover, and refrigerate for up to 8 hours before serving.

To serve, divide the lemon slices between the 2 pitchers, then add a generous amount of ice cubes to each pitcher. Using a wooden spoon, stir the mixture to combine. Serve in tall glasses.

SERVES 10
10 MINUTES PREPARATION

fill an assortment of decoratively shaped ice-cube trays with water and put them in the freezer. If you like, use purified water for clearer, cleaner-tasting ice.

pop the ice cubes out of the trays, put them in a freezer bag, and put the bag in the freezer. Then refill the trays and make more cubes until you have as many as you need.

place the cubes in an ice bucket or an attractive bowl, with a scoop or tongs so guests can help themselves and add to lemonade or other beverages. Restock the ice cubes as needed throughout the afternoon.

grilled sausages, portobello mushrooms, and onions

15 MINUTES
PREPARATION

20 MINUTES
COOKING

SERVING TIP

A condiment tray is not only colorful but also presents an easy way for guests to help themselves to what they like. Spoon your assorted condiments into small bowls and then arrange the bowls on one or more serving trays.

Precooked sausages made from beef, pork, lamb, or poultry and flavored with a variety of seasonings are sold vacuum-packed in the meat department of many markets. A selection of three or four different kinds is perfect for a crowd. For vegetarians, offer grilled portobello mushrooms and red onions. Provide guests with freshly grilled rolls and a selection of condiments to assemble their own sandwiches.

Prepare a charcoal or gas grill for direct grilling over medium heat. Lightly brush the sausages and cut sides of the ciabatta rolls with ¼ cup (2 fl oz/60 ml) of the olive oil. Grill the sausages, turning once, until heated through and slightly charred, about 4 minutes on each side. Transfer the sausages to a cutting board.

In a bowl, whisk together the remaining ½ cup (4 fl oz/125 ml) olive oil, the balsamic vinegar, garlic, and thyme. Season to taste with salt and pepper. Brush the mushroom caps and onion slices with the olive oil mixture, coating them evenly. Grill the mushrooms and onions, turning once, until they are soft and lightly charred, about 3 minutes on each side. Place the ciabatta rolls cut side down on the grate and grill until lightly toasted and warm, about 2 minutes.

While the vegetables and rolls are on the grill, cut the sausages on the diagonal into thirds. Capture any carving juices, if possible. Arrange the sausage pieces on a warmed serving platter. Drizzle any carving juices over the sausages. Arrange the mushrooms and onions alongside the sausages or on another warmed platter, and garnish with rosemary sprigs, if desired. Serve at once, with the ciabatta rolls and condiments.

SERVES 10

5 lb (2.5 kg) assorted precooked sausages, at room temperature

10 ciabatta rolls, split in half

¾ cup (6 fl oz/180 ml) olive oil

¼ cup (2 fl oz/60 ml) balsamic vinegar

1 clove garlic, finely chopped

1 tablespoon fresh thyme leaves

Coarse salt and freshly ground pepper

10 portobello mushrooms, 5 inches (13 cm) in diameter, brushed clean and stems removed

3 red onions, sliced ¼ inch (6 mm) thick

Assorted condiments such as pickle relish, tomato relish, onion jam, pesto, crumbled fresh goat cheese, flavored mustards and mayonnaises, and sliced tomatoes

Fresh rosemary sprigs for garnish (optional)

pasta salad with grilled vegetables

TOMATO VINAIGRETTE

$1/2$ cup (4 fl oz/125 ml) prepared marinara sauce

$1/2$ cup (4 fl oz/125 ml) olive oil

$1/3$ cup (3 fl oz/90 ml) red wine vinegar

Salt and freshly ground pepper

1 lb (500 g) penne or other tube-shaped pasta

1–2 tablespoons olive oil

1 lb (500 g) prepared assorted grilled vegetables, coarsely chopped

1 tablespoon capers

$1/4$ cup ($1/3$ oz/10 g) torn fresh basil leaves

The secret of this easy salad is to buy grilled vegetables at a good supermarket deli or specialty-food store.

To make the vinaigrette, in a small bowl, whisk together the marinara sauce, olive oil, and vinegar. Season to taste with salt and pepper. Set aside.

Bring a large pot three-fourths full of salted water to a boil over high heat. Add the pasta, stir well, and cook until al dente, about 10 minutes, or according to package directions. Drain the pasta, refresh under cold water, and then drain again thoroughly. Toss the pasta with a little olive oil to keep it from sticking.

Combine the pasta and grilled vegetables in a large bowl. (The salad can be prepared up to this point, covered, and refrigerated for up to 12 hours.) Just before serving, add the vinaigrette and toss to coat evenly. To serve, transfer the pasta salad to a serving platter and garnish with the capers and basil.

SERVES 10

15 MINUTES PREPARATION

10 MINUTES COOKING

RECIPE TIP
Look for grilled vegetables at the prepared foods counter of the market. Use any of the following: zucchini (courgette), fennel, eggplant (aubergine), onions, bell peppers (capsicums), corn, and asparagus.

cherry tomato, parmesan, and arugula salad

2 bags (6 oz/185 g each) arugula (rocket)

1 basket (8 oz/250 g) Sweet 100 cherry tomatoes or grape tomatoes

1 container (4 oz/125 g) Parmesan cheese shavings

1 large lemon

$1/4$ cup (2 fl oz/60 ml) extra-virgin olive oil

Coarse salt and freshly ground pepper

Tiny Sweet 100 cherry tomatoes are ideal for this recipe. If they are not available, cut grape tomatoes in half. Baby spinach leaves can be combined with the arugula for a more mellow flavor.

In a large salad bowl, combine the arugula, tomatoes, and Parmesan shavings.

Cut the lemon in half and squeeze the juice over the salad, discarding any seeds. Drizzle with the olive oil and season to taste with salt and pepper. Toss to coat. Spoon out the salad directly from the bowl or mound the freshly dressed salad on a large serving platter. Serve at once.

SERVES 10

10 MINUTES PREPARATION

INGREDIENT TIP
Look for preshaved Parmesan in the specialty cheese section of the grocery store, or make your own shavings using a vegetable peeler and a wedge of Parmesan.

sandwich picnic

tips and shopping notes

- Slip assorted bakery or store-bought cookies into individual plastic gift bags and tie with twine or ribbon.

- Pack drinks in tightly capped Mason jars that can double as drinking glasses. Brightly colored striped straws are a fun accent.

- Real plates are a fitting match for this menu. Stack them along the side of the basket, then snugly nestle in the food and drinks to hold the plates in place.

- Make individual bundles of cutlery and cloth napkins and secure them with twine.

- For wine, serve a light Beaujolais for a red and a well-chilled Pinot Grigio for a white.

work plan

IN ADVANCE

Mix the cranberry limeade

Make the sandwiches

Make the white bean salad

Prepare the dressing for the broccoli slaw

Pack the cookies into bags

JUST BEFORE SERVING

Make the broccoli slaw

Pack the picnic basket

menu

Cranberry Limeade

•

*Focaccia with Havarti, Arugula,
and Eggplant Spread*

•

*Baguette with French Ham, Gruyère,
and Cornichons*

•

Artichoke and White Bean Salad

•

Broccoli Slaw with Pine Nuts

•

Assorted Cookies

write out labels for the sandwiches you will be serving. Look for a charming, old-fashioned style with a decorative border at a good stationery store.

wrap each sandwich in an individual waxed-paper bag (available at restaurant-supply stores and many markets), or in a piece of parchment (baking) paper.

attach the labels to the sandwiches, using them to secure the wrapping. Place the sandwiches in a basket with the labels facing up, so guests can help themselves.

sandwiches to go

Waxed-paper bags secured closed with labels provide an easy and stylish way to transport sandwiches—and for guests to select their sandwich choice. For added protection during the journey, place the wrapped sandwiches into a smaller basket.

french ham
&
gruyere

cranberry limeade

5 MINUTES
PREPARATION

SERVING TIP
If you don't have
Mason or jelly jars on
hand, transfer the
drink to a thermos
and refrigerate until
ready to transport.
Serve over ice in
tall glasses.

Pack and tote beverages in individual spillproof containers that guests can drink from directly. If prepared limeade is not available, use frozen limeade concentrate mixed as directed on the package.

In a large mixing bowl, combine the limeade, cranberry juice, and lime slices and stir until blended. Ladle the mixture into eight 1½-cup (12–fl oz/375-ml) Mason jars with screw caps. Keep refrigerated until ready to serve. To serve, place a few ice cubes and a straw in each jar and pass to each guest.

SERVES 8

2 qt (2 l) prepared limeade

2 cups (16 fl oz/500 ml) cranberry juice

2 limes, thinly sliced

Ice cubes for serving

focaccia with havarti, arugula, and eggplant spread

1 focaccia bread, about 7 by 12 inches (18 by 30 cm)

1 container (15 oz/470 g) baba ghanoush or other roasted eggplant (aubergine) spread

1/2 lb (250 g) Havarti cheese, thinly sliced

2 cups (2 oz/60 g) arugula (rocket) leaves

1/2 cup (2 1/2 oz/75 g) sun-dried tomatoes packed in oil, drained and julienned

Freshly ground pepper

For a variation, substitute pesto for the eggplant spread and smoked fontina or pepper jack for the Havarti. This recipe also works well when grilled in a panini-style sandwich press.

On a cutting board, using a serrated knife, cut the focaccia in half horizontally. Spread the baba ghanoush evenly over the cut side of the bottom half of the focaccia. Top with a layer of the cheese, followed by a layer of the arugula, and then the sun-dried tomatoes. Season to taste with pepper. Cover with the top half of the focaccia, cut side down. Cut the sandwich into 8 equal portions. Place each portion in a waxed-paper bag and seal the bag with an adhesive label. Refrigerate until serving.

SERVES 8

10 MINUTES PREPARATION

MAKE-AHEAD TIP Place each sandwich portion in a waxed-paper bag, seal with an adhesive label, and refrigerate for up to 4 hours.

baguette with french ham, gruyère, and cornichons

1 long baguette

2 tablespoons unsalted butter, at room temperature

2 tablespoons Dijon mustard

1/2 lb (250 g) French ham, sliced paper-thin

6 oz (185 g) Gruyère cheese, thinly sliced

8 cornichons, thinly sliced lengthwise

French ham, also sold as jambon de Paris, *is a delicately flavored cooked ham that is best eaten cold.*

Using a serrated knife, cut the baguette in half horizontally. Spread the butter evenly over the cut side of the bottom half of the baguette, and spread the mustard evenly over the cut side of the top half.

Layer the ham slices on the bottom baguette half, followed by a layer of the cheese slices, and then the cornichons. Cover with the top half of the baguette, pressing down gently so that the sandwich holds together. Cut the sandwich crosswise into 8 equal portions. Place each portion in a waxed-paper bag and seal the bag with an adhesive label. Refrigerate until serving.

SERVES 8

10 MINUTES PREPARATION

SHOPPING TIP Look for French ham *(jambon de Paris)* at specialty-deli counters and many well-stocked markets. If you can't find it, substitute any lightly salted, nonsmoked sandwich ham.

artichoke and white bean salad

15 MINUTES
PREPARATION

30 MINUTES
RESTING

MAKE-AHEAD TIP
The salad can
be prepared in
advance, covered,
and refrigerated
for up to 24 hours.
Remove from
the refrigerator
30 minutes
before serving.

For extra flavor, sprinkle the artichoke hearts with olive oil, salt, and pepper, and roast for 15 minutes in a preheated 400°F (200°C) oven. For a variation, add one jar (10 ½ oz/330 g) Italian tuna packed in oil.

To make the dressing, in a small bowl, whisk together the olive oil, lemon juice, garlic, mustard, red pepper flakes, and fennel seeds. Season to taste with salt and pepper. Let stand for at least 30 minutes or for up to 4 hours, to allow the flavors to blend.

In a large bowl, combine the artichoke hearts, beans, onion, celery, and oregano. Add the dressing and toss to coat the salad evenly. Transfer the salad to a serving bowl or, for transporting, pack in an airtight container.

SERVES 8

DRESSING

$1/2$ cup (4 fl oz/125 ml) olive oil

$1/4$ cup (2 fl oz/60 ml) fresh lemon juice

1 clove garlic, thinly sliced

1 teaspoon Dijon mustard

$1/4$ teaspoon red pepper flakes

1 teaspoon ground fennel seeds

Salt and freshly ground pepper

1 package (8 oz/250 g) frozen quartered artichoke hearts, thawed

2 cans (15 oz/470 g each) white (navy) beans, rinsed and drained

1 small red onion, diced

2 celery stalks, thinly sliced

2 tablespoons chopped fresh oregano

broccoli slaw with pine nuts

10 MINUTES
PREPARATION

MAKE-AHEAD TIP
The dressing can
be prepared in
advance, covered,
and refrigerated for
up to 24 hours.

To make this easy side dish, use a packaged slaw mix of broccoli, carrots, and cabbage or a traditional cabblage slaw blend. (See photograph on page 62.)

To make the dressing, in a small bowl, whisk together the mayonnaise, mustard, and vinegar. Season to taste with salt and pepper.

In a large bowl, combine the broccoli slaw mix, currants, parsley, and pine nuts. Add the dressing and toss to coat the salad evenly. Transfer the salad to a serving bowl or, for transporting, pack in an airtight container.

SERVES 8

DRESSING

$1/2$ cup (4 fl oz/125 ml) mayonnaise

2 tablespoons coarse-grain mustard

$1/4$ cup (2 fl oz/60 ml) cider vinegar

Salt and freshly ground pepper

2 packages (1 lb/500 g each) broccoli slaw mix

$1/2$ cup (3 oz/90 g) dried currants

$1/2$ cup ($3/4$ oz/20 g) chopped fresh flat-leaf (Italian) parsley

$1/2$ cup ($2 1/2$ oz/75 g) pine nuts, toasted

evening

dinner party

tips and shopping notes

- As the guests arrive, pass flutes of chilled Prosecco (Italian sparkling wine) on a napkin-lined tray.

- Set the table with good-quality linens and silverware and plain white plates that showcase the food.

- Use slender white candles at varying heights to create a warm, welcoming mood.

- Keep decorations natural: bouquets of tea roses on the table and sideboard; a few lemon leaves to decorate a butter plate or garnish a tray.

- Buy crushed ice for serving the oysters.

- For wine, serve a Mersault or a Montrachet for a red and a not-too-oaky Chardonnay or a Sauvignon Blanc for a white.

work plan

IN ADVANCE

Prepare the mignonette and the vinaigrette

Make the chive butter

Combine the salad greens

Rub the asparagus with lemon butter

Assemble the chocolate espresso crèmes

JUST BEFORE SERVING

Assemble the oyster tray and charcuterie platter

Roast the asparagus and the halibut

Toss the salad

Whip the cream and garnish the dessert

menu

Prosecco

•

Oysters on the Half Shell with
Green Peppercorn Mignonette

•

Charcuterie Plate
with Radishes and Butter

•

Frisée, Endive, and Watercress Salad
with Roquefort and Pear

•

Roasted Asparagus

•

Roasted Halibut with Chive
Butter and Caviar

•

Chocolate Espresso Crèmes
with Candied Orange Peel

fold unadorned white cards (you can use store-bought place cards, or make your own using heavy card stock). Write guests' names on the cards in an ink color that complements the setting.

tie a thin silver ribbon or string around the fold of each card and secure with a knot, allowing the ends to hang down and curl.

place a simply folded napkin on the plate at each setting, and set the cards on top of the napkins.

easy place cards

Place cards are more than a decorative touch. They let you create an ideal seating plan that puts guests where they will be most comfortable, while relieving them of the pressure of deciding where to sit.

oysters on the half shell with green peppercorn mignonette

10 MINUTES
PREPARATION

SHOPPING TIP
When ordering the oysters, ask your fishmonger to shuck them and then pack them on ice.

Order oysters from your favorite fish counter for pickup on the day of your party. Select a couple of different varieties, such as Kumamoto and Malpeque, both of which are small and have a sweet liquor that will complement the Prosecco.

To make the mignonette sauce, in a small bowl, stir together the vinegar, lemon juice, shallot, and peppercorns. Season to taste with salt. Cover and refrigerate until serving. (The sauce can be prepared in advance, covered, and refrigerated for up to 24 hours.)

To serve, cover a large metal serving tray with crushed ice. Arrange the shucked oysters on the tray, nestling the shells in the ice. Transfer the sauce to a small serving bowl and nestle it in the ice on the tray with the oysters. Place a spoon into the sauce and serve at once.

MIGNONETTE

$2/3$ cup (5 fl oz/160 ml) white wine vinegar

2 tablespoons fresh lemon juice

1 tablespoon finely chopped shallot

1 tablespoon drained brined green peppercorns, chopped

Coarse salt

Crushed ice

18 oysters, shucked

charcuterie plate with radishes and butter

10 MINUTES
PREPARATION

SHOPPING TIP
If you can't find long, slender, two-toned French radishes, regular round red radishes can be substituted.

Purchase the pâté a day in advance and keep it refrigerated until ready to serve. Order it presliced, with the slices separated by waxed paper. Country-style pâté is usually made from pork, but some specialty stores carry a similar coarse pâté made from poultry.

Place 2 pâté slices on each individual chilled salad plate. Garnish each serving with 2 radishes, 3 cornichons, 1 tablespoon of the mustard, a piece of butter, and 1½ teaspoons of the salt. Serve at once, alongside the baguette.

EACH RECIPE SERVES 6

12 slices country-style pâté, each cut ¼ inch (6 mm) thick

12 French radishes, trimmed

18 cornichons

6 tablespoons (3 oz/90 g) Dijon mustard

½ cup (4 oz/125 g) unsalted butter, cut into 6 pieces

3 tablespoons coarse salt

1 baguette, sliced

frisée, endive, and watercress salad with roquefort and pear

PEAR VINAIGRETTE

2 tablespoons Champagne vinegar

6 tablespoons (3 fl oz/90 ml) toasted walnut oil

1/2 teaspoon honey

1 firm but ripe pear such as Anjou or Bartlett (Williams'), peeled, cored, and cut into 1/4-inch (6-mm) dice

Salt and freshly ground pepper

1 head frisée, cored and torn into bite-sized pieces

2 heads Belgian endive (chicory/witloof), cored and cut lengthwise into narrow strips

1 bunch young, tender watercress, tough stems removed

6 oz (185 g) Roquefort cheese

Ideally, purchase salad greens on the same day you plan to eat them to ensure that they stay crisp and fresh. Combine the greens in a bowl an hour before serving, cover with a damp paper towel, and refrigerate until you are ready to dress the salad and serve.

To make the vinaigrette, in a small bowl, whisk together the vinegar, walnut oil, and honey. Stir in the pear. Season to taste with salt and pepper. Let stand at room temperature for at least 30 minutes or up to 4 hours.

In a large bowl, combine the frisée, endive, and watercress. Whisk the vinaigrette, drizzle it over the greens, and toss to coat the leaves well. Cut the Roquefort cheese into 6 slices. To serve, divide the greens evenly among chilled individual plates and top each with a slice of Roquefort. Serve at once.

SERVES 6

10 MINUTES PREPARATION

SHOPPING TIP Other blue-veined cheeses can be substituted for the Roquefort, such as Gorgonzola, Cabrales, or Cambozola.

roasted asparagus

1 1/2 lb (750 g) thin asparagus spears, tough ends removed

4 tablespoons (2 oz/60 g) unsalted butter, at room temperature

1 tablespoon grated lemon zest

Coarse salt and freshly ground pepper

Seek out thin asparagus spears for an elegant presentation. If making ahead, bring to room temperature, season with salt and pepper, and roast as directed. (See photograph on page 76.)

Preheat the oven to 450°F (230°C). Place the asparagus on a rimmed baking sheet large enough to hold them in a single layer. In a small bowl, using a fork, combine the butter and lemon zest. With your hands, rub the asparagus with the lemon butter until evenly coated. Season with salt and pepper. Roast until lightly browned but still crisp, about 10 minutes. To serve, place a few asparagus on each individual plate and drizzle any pan juices over the top. Serve at once.

SERVES 6

10 MINUTES PREPARATION

10 MINUTES COOKING

MAKE-AHEAD TIP The asparagus can be rubbed with the lemon butter a day in advance, covered, and refrigerated.

roasted halibut with chive butter and caviar

15 MINUTES
PREPARATION

8 MINUTES
COOKING

SHOPPING TIP
If you can't find
halibut, substitute
sturgeon, sea bass,
or turbot fillets.

When buying fish, ask for fillets that are uniform in size and weight; order in advance, so that they are ready for pickup when you arrive.

To make the chive butter, in a food processor, combine the butter, chopped chives, lemon juice, and ¼ teaspoon pepper and pulse until the chives are evenly distributed throughout the butter. Using a rubber spatula, scrape the chive butter onto a piece of plastic wrap and form into a log. Refrigerate for at least 30 minutes or up to 24 hours to blend the flavors.

Preheat the oven to 450°F (230°C). Pat the halibut fillets dry with paper towels and place the fillets on a nonstick rimmed baking sheet. Brush the fillets with the olive oil and season with salt and pepper. Roast the fillets until they start to turn golden and are just opaque at the center when tested with a knife, about 8 minutes.

While the fish is roasting, remove the chive butter from the refrigerator and cut the log into 6 equal pieces. Set aside.

To serve, place 1 halibut fillet in the center of each warmed individual plate and top with a pat of the chive butter. Spoon a dollop of the caviar onto each serving and garnish with a sprinkle of chives. Place a bundle of roasted asparagus spears (page 82) alongside the fish. Serve at once.

SERVES 6

CHIVE BUTTER

½ cup (4 oz/125 g) unsalted butter, at room temperature

¼ cup (½ oz/15 g) chopped fresh chives

1 tablespoon fresh lemon juice

¼ teaspoon freshly ground pepper

6 halibut fillets, each 6 oz (185 g) and about 1½ inches (4 cm) thick

3 tablespoons olive oil

Coarse salt and freshly ground pepper

1 oz (30 g) osetra or sevruga caviar or American paddlefish roe

10 fresh chives, cut into 2-inch (5-cm) lengths

chocolate espresso crèmes with candied orange peel

For this remarkably easy and ultradecadent treat, use bittersweet chocolate containing at least 70 percent cacao. You can also flavor the whipped cream with a touch of vanilla extract (essence). Use demitasse spoons for serving.

2 cups (16 fl oz/500 ml) heavy (double) cream

6 oz (185 g) bittersweet chocolate, finely chopped

1 tablespoon instant espresso powder

Candied orange peel, cut into narrow strips, for garnish

In a large saucepan over medium-high heat, bring 1½ cups (12 fl oz/375 ml) of the cream almost to a boil, until bubbles start to form on the surface. Remove from the heat and stir in the chocolate and espresso powder. Using a whisk, beat vigorously until the chocolate is melted and the mixture is silky smooth, about 1 minute. Divide the mixture evenly among 6 demitasse cups or ⅓-cup (30–fl oz/80-ml) ramekins. Cover loosely with plastic wrap and refrigerate until well chilled and the edges are firm, at least 6 hours or up to 24 hours. Remove from the refrigerator 15 minutes before serving.

To serve, in a bowl, using an electric mixer or a whisk, whip the remaining ½ cup (4 fl oz/125 ml) cream until soft peaks form. Garnish each dessert with a dollop of whipped cream and a few strips of orange peel.

SERVES 6

15 MINUTES PREPARATION

10 MINUTES COOKING

SHOPPING TIP
Look for candied orange peel in the bulk bins of most grocery stores or in confectionery or cake-decorating specialty shops.

cocktail party

tips and shopping notes

- Serve two signature cocktails, one without alcohol, and supplement them with a self-serve bar that includes wine, sparkling water, juice, soft drinks, and plenty of ice.

- Set up the bar in the kitchen on an island or a table. Keeping the bar close to water and refrigeration will make it easier to restock throughout the party.

- Decorate disposable coasters and paper napkins with a rubber stamp that reflects the theme of the party.

- Votives add sparkle to the table, bar, and mantel—even at an afternoon party.

- Purchase roasted and salted nuts, such as almonds or walnuts, and place in bowls.

menu

Limoncello Martinis

•

Citrus Mint Cocktails

•

Marinated Feta Cubes and Stuffed Olives

•

Fig and Goat Cheese Canapés

•

Oven-Roasted Pesto Shrimp Skewers

•

Bacon and Asiago Scone Bites

work plan

IN ADVANCE

Make the canapés

Prepare the shrimp skewers

Bake the scone bites

JUST BEFORE SERVING

Mix the cocktails

Assemble the feta and olives

Roast the shrimp skewers

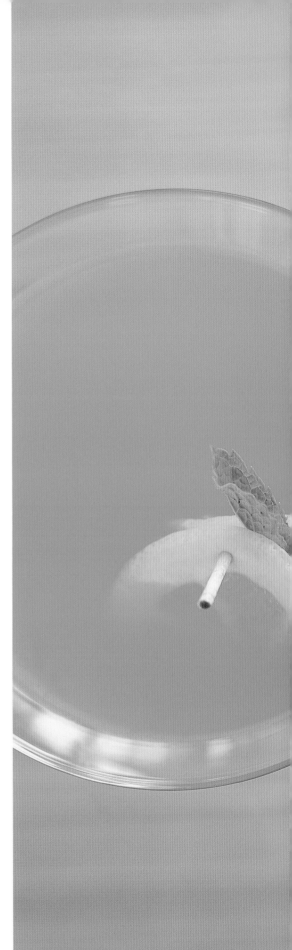

cut strips of lemon peel, about ½ inch (12 mm) wide, using a sharp paring knife. Roll the strips into curls; use a toothpick to hold the curl in place if preparing in advance. Hang a curl on the edge of each glass.

use a bar-style lemon stripper to cut uniform strips of lemon peel about 4 inches (10 cm) long. Tie each strip into a loose knot. Float in the drink.

place a decorative pick through a folded thin lemon slice. Tuck a tiny fresh mint sprig inside the slice. Float in the drink or balance on the glass rim.

drink garnishes

A garnish can turn any drink into a sophisticated cocktail. Here are three easy ideas for the drinks on this menu. Prepare the garnishes in advance and refrigerate, covered with a damp paper towel.

limoncello martinis

5 MINUTES
PREPARATION

MIXING TIP
A few lemon
slices in the
shaker will add
a pleasant flavor.

When making cocktails, use ice made from purified distilled water instead of tap water to avoid off flavors. The crystal-clear appearance of purified ice will also add a sparkle to your drinks.

Put 6 martini glasses in the freezer to chill for at least 15 minutes. Just before serving, fill a cocktail shaker half full with ice. Working in two batches, pour over half of the limoncello and half of the gin. Cover with the lid and shake vigorously for about 10 seconds. Strain into the chilled glasses, dividing evenly. Garnish each glass with a lemon twist. Serve at once.

SERVES 6

Ice cubes

1 cup (8 fl oz/250 ml) limoncello liqueur

1 cup (8 fl oz/250 ml) gin

6 lemon twists

citrus mint cocktails

10 MINUTES
PREPARATION

Always include a nonalcoholic cocktail on the drink menu. Serve it in an elegant cocktail glass and garnish it with style.

Put 6 martini glasses in the freezer to chill for at least 15 minutes. Just before serving, fill a cocktail shaker half full with ice. Working in two batches, pour over half of the lemonade, lime juice, and mint syrup. Cover with the lid and shake vigorously for about 10 seconds. Strain into the chilled glasses, dividing evenly. Garnish each glass with a lemon twist and a mint sprig. Serve at once.

SERVES 6

Ice cubes

1 1/2 cups (12 fl oz/375 ml) prepared lemonade

1/2 cup (4 fl oz/125 ml) fresh lime juice

1/4 cup (2 fl oz/60 ml) mint-flavored syrup

6 lemon twists

6 fresh mint sprigs

marinated feta cubes

The tangy, salty flavor of feta cheese is a perfect match for cocktails. Buy jars of precut feta cubes packed in olive oil with herbs and garlic. Mini marinated mozzarella balls are also readily available and can be served alongside, or in place of, the feta cubes.

2 jars (10 1/2 oz/330 g each) marinated feta cheese cubes

Extra-virgin olive oil for drizzling

Drain the feta cubes in a colander. To serve, transfer the feta to a plate or shallow serving bowl. Drizzle the feta with olive oil. Place a toothpick in each cube, or fill a shot glass with toothpicks and place it in the center of the bowl with the feta cubes arranged around it. Include an empty bowl alongside, so that guests can discard the used toothpicks; place a toothpick in the bowl to indicate its use.

SERVES 12

5 MINUTES PREPARATION

SHOPPING TIP
If you opt for small mozzarella balls, look for containers labeled marinated *bocconcini*.

stuffed olives

For an hors d'oeuvre that is both easy to serve and eat, buy a variety of stuffed olives, either in jars or scooped from crocks.

1 container (8 oz/250 g) stuffed green olives, 2 or 3 types

Drain the olives in a colander. To serve, divide each olive variety among a few small serving bowls, and then create a cluster of bowls, one with each variety, at different points around the room where guests tend to congregate. Put toothpicks and a stack of cocktail napkins nearby. Include an empty bowl for discarded toothpicks, too, and place a toothpick in the bowl to indicate its use.

SERVES 12

5 MINUTES PREPARATION

SHOPPING TIP
Look for large green olives filled with whole blanched almonds, slivers of sun-dried tomatoes, rolled anchovy fillets, or Gorgonzola cheese morsels.

fig and goat cheese canapés

15 MINUTES
PREPARATION

INGREDIENT TIP
To make the goat
cheese easier to
crumble, put it in the
freezer for 15 minutes
before crumbling.

Make these in summer, when figs are in season. Black Mission, Kadota, and Adriactic varieties are good choices. Pre-made baguette crostini are available from specialty bakers and well-stocked food stores.

Spread each of the crostini evenly with 2 teaspoons of the fig spread. Sprinkle the goat cheese over the fig spread, and drape a piece of the prosciutto over the top. (The canapés can be prepared up to this point, covered with plastic wrap, and refrigerated for up to 4 hours.) Garnish each canapé with a fig slice, if desired. Arrange on a platter and serve at once.

MAKES 24 CANAPÉS; SERVES 12

24 store-bought toasted
baguette crostini

1 jar (8 oz/250 g) fig spread

1/4 lb (125 g) fresh goat cheese,
crumbled

3 oz (90 g) thinly sliced
prosciutto, torn into 24 pieces

4 figs, each cut into 6 slices
(optional)

oven-roasted pesto shrimp skewers

15 MINUTES
PREPARATION

10 MINUTES
COOKING

Buying peeled, deveined shrimp and prepared pesto saves prep time and cleanup in the kitchen.

Position a rack in the upper third of the oven and preheat to 400°F (200°C). Line a large baking sheet with parchment (baking) paper. Soak 30 small wooden skewers in water to cover for 10 minutes and then drain.

In a bowl, combine the shrimp and pesto and toss until the shrimp are evenly coated. Thread 2 shrimp onto each skewer. (The skewers can be prepared up to this point, covered with plastic wrap, and refrigerated for up to 24 hours.)

Arrange the skewers in a single layer on the prepared baking sheet. Sprinkle with the red pepper flakes. Roast the shrimp until just opaque throughout, 8–10 minutes. Transfer the shrimp skewers to a warmed platter. Serve at once.

MAKES 30 SKEWERS; SERVES 12

1 package (2 lb/1 kg) frozen
uncooked peeled and deveined
medium shrimp (prawns),
about 60 total, thawed

1 container (7 oz/220 g) prepared
pesto

1/2 teaspoon red pepper flakes

bacon and asiago scone bites

3 slices bacon

2 cups (10 oz/315 g) all-purpose (plain) flour

1 tablespoon baking powder

1 container (5 oz/155 g) grated Asiago cheese, about 1¼ cups

½ teaspoon freshly ground pepper

½ cup (4 oz/125 g) chilled unsalted butter, cut into small pieces

1 large egg

½ cup (4 fl oz/125 ml) heavy (double) cream

The idea for these filling bites is borrowed from breakfast, but the addition of Asiago cheese and bacon turns the typical scone dough into perfect cocktail fare. Look for pint containers of grated Asiago cheese in the cheese section of most markets.

Preheat the oven to 400°F (200°C). Line a large baking sheet with parchment (baking) paper.

Lay the bacon slices in a single layer in a cold frying pan. Place the pan over medium heat and cook until the edges of the slices start to curl and the bacon starts to brown, about 3 minutes. Using kitchen tongs, turn the bacon slices over and cook until browned, about 3 minutes longer. Transfer the bacon to a plate lined with paper towels to drain briefly, and then transfer to a cutting board and chop finely. Set aside.

In a food processor, combine the flour, baking powder, Asiago cheese, and pepper and pulse briefly to mix. Add the butter and pulse until the mixture resembles coarse meal. In a small bowl, whisk together the egg and cream until blended. Pour the egg mixture into the processor and pulse just until the dough comes together.

Turn the dough out onto a lightly floured work surface. Knead in the chopped bacon and bring the dough together into a ball. Using a floured rolling pin, roll out the dough into an 8-inch (20-cm) square about ½ inch (12 mm) thick. Using a sharp knife, cut the dough into 1-inch (2.5-cm) squares.

Transfer the squares to the prepared baking sheet, spacing them evenly. Bake the squares until golden, about 15 minutes. Transfer to a wire rack and let cool for at least 15 minutes before serving.

MAKES 64 PIECES; SERVES 12

15 MINUTES PREPARATION

20 MINUTES COOKING

MAKE-AHEAD TIPS The dough can be prepared in advance and refrigerated for up to 24 hours; remove from the refrigerator 15 minutes before baking. The scone bites can be baked in advance and stored in an airtight container for up to 24 hours.

celebratory buffet

work plan

IN ADVANCE

Prepare the shrimp spread

Assemble the gratin

Blanch the green beans

Assemble the pudding

BEFORE SERVING

Mix the fruit punch

Roast the pork

Bake the gratin

Roast the carrots

Sauté the green beans

Whip the cream

tips and shopping notes

- For the buffet, choose a table or sideboard just big enough to hold everything, so the menu looks abundant.

- Make sure there is plenty of space around the buffet for easy access.

- Set the plates at the start of the buffet. Place napkins and silverware at the end, so guests won't have to juggle them as they help themselves to the food.

- Roll forks and knives in napkins, which makes them easier to pick up and carry.

- A punch bowl and self-serve dip tray are two good ways to accommodate a crowd.

- For wine, serve a Merlot or Cabernet Sauvignon for a red and a Chardonnay or Viognier for a white.

menu

Pineapple Ginger Ale Fruit Punch

•

Shrimp and Green Onion Spread

•

*Roasted Pork Loin with
Sweet Onions and Apples*

•

Potato and Cheddar Gratin

•

Roasted Carrots with Orange Zest

•

*Sautéed Green Beans with
Almonds and Mustard Butter*

•

*Berry Shortcake Pudding with
Whipped Cream*

pineapple ginger ale fruit punch

5 MINUTES
PREPARATION

SERVING TIP
Place the punch
bowl on a small side
table so guests can
access it easily.

Create a festive—and easy—punch by combining ginger ale with fruit juice and sliced fresh fruits. Orange, apple, and cranberry juices will also work well in place of the pineapple juice, as will more unusual choices, such as coconut, mango, and pear.

Fill a large glass punch bowl half full with ice. Add the pineapple juice, ginger ale, orange slices, lime slices, and pineapple chunks. Stir to combine the ingredients. To serve, ladle the punch into glasses and garnish each glass with a mint sprig. If desired, add a shot of rum to each glass. Serve at once.

SERVES 12

Ice cubes

2 qt (2 l) unsweetened pineapple juice, chilled

2 qt (2 l) ginger ale, chilled

1 navel orange, thinly sliced

2 limes, thinly sliced

1 container (8 oz/250 g) fresh pineapple chunks

Fresh mint sprigs for garnish

Dark rum (optional)

shrimp and green onion spread

15 MINUTES
PREPARATION

SHOPPING TIP
Buy precut celery
hearts to save time.

This flavorful dip can also be served warm—simply cover and heat in the microwave on medium-high power for 30 seconds. For a variation, use crabmeat instead of shrimp. You can also serve this dip with bread sticks, flat breads, or crackers.

In a food processor, combine the shrimp, cream cheese, green onions, salt, pepper, and Tabasco and Worcestershire sauces. Pulse until smooth and creamy. (The spread can be prepared up to this point, transferred to a container, covered, and refrigerated for up to 24 hours.)

When ready to serve, transfer the spread to a small bowl. Arrange the bowl and celery sticks on a serving platter. Serve at once.

SERVES 12

1 lb (500 g) cooked bay shrimp (prawns), drained

1 container (8 oz/250 g) whipped cream cheese

4 green (spring) onions, including tender green tops, chopped

1/4 teaspoon coarse salt

1/2 teaspoon freshly ground pepper

2 dashes of Tabasco sauce

2 dashes of Worcestershire sauce

1 container (14 oz/440 g) prepared celery sticks

roasted pork loin with sweet onions and apples

4 tablespoons (2 oz/60 g) unsalted butter, at room temperature

2 tablespoons Dijon mustard

2 tablespoons dried sage

1 tablespoon coarse salt

2 teaspoons freshly ground pepper

1 boneless pork loin roast, 6–6 1/2 lb (3–3.25 kg), tied

2 Vidalia or other sweet onions, each cut into 8 wedges

2 Golden Delicious apples, cored and each cut into 8 wedges

Fresh sage sprigs for garnish (optional)

Roasting a well-seasoned boneless pork loin is a great way to feed a crowd. Much like a ham, it is fine served at room temperature, making it a good choice for a buffet.

In a small bowl, stir together the butter, mustard, sage, salt, and pepper to form a paste. Smear the paste over the entire roast, coating it evenly. Let the roast stand at room temperature for 1 hour.

Preheat the oven to 450°F (230°C).

Place the pork loin, fat side facing up, in a roasting pan with the onion and apple wedges along the sides. Roast for 15 minutes. Gently toss the onion and apple wedges to coat them in the pan juices. Reduce the oven temperature to 350°F (180°C) and continue to roast until an instant-read thermometer inserted into the thickest part of the pork loin registers 160°F (71°C), about 1 hour and 20 minutes longer. Transfer the pork to a cutting board, tent with aluminum foil, and let rest for 10 minutes. Reserve the pan.

To serve, carve the pork into slices 1/4 inch (6 mm) thick. Arrange the pork slices and the onion and apple wedges on a warmed serving platter. Spoon any juices from the roasting pan or carving board over the top. Serve at once.

SERVES 12

10 MINUTES PREPARATION

95 MINUTES COOKING

RECIPE TIP
For a variation, roast wedges of Bosc or Anjou pear alongside the pork loin in place of the apples.

potato and cheddar gratin

10 MINUTES
PREPARATION

1 HOUR
COOKING

*This hearty dish nicely rounds out any buffet menu. For a
variation, use Gruyère in place of the Cheddar and stir in 1 cup
(6 oz/185 g) diced cooked ham when combining the ingredients.*

Preheat the oven to 375°F (190°C). Butter two attractive 2-qt (2-l) shallow
baking dishes.

Measure out ½ cup (2 oz/60 g) of the cheese and reserve for garnishing the
top of the gratin. In a large bowl, combine the potatoes, onion, and
remaining 3½ cups (14 oz/440 g) cheese. Stir in the salt, pepper, half-and-
half, and milk. Divide the mixture evenly between the prepared baking
dishes, spreading it in an even layer. Sprinkle the reserved cheese over the
top and lightly dust each gratin with half of the nutmeg.

Cover the baking dishes with aluminum foil and bake for 40 minutes. Remove
the foil and continue to bake until the tops are golden, 15–20 minutes longer.
Remove from the oven and let cool for 10 minutes before serving.

SERVES 12

COOKING TIPS
Assemble the gratin
the evening before,
cover, and refrigerate
until 15 minutes
before baking. Cook
the gratin and the
roasted carrots first
and wrap them in foil;
return both dishes to
the oven during the
last 10 minutes of
cooking the pork
to reheat.

1 package (1 lb/500 g)
preshredded sharp Cheddar
cheese, about 4 cups

3 packages (18 oz/560g each)
precut precooked shredded
potatoes

1 yellow onion, finely chopped

1 teaspoon coarse salt

1 teaspoon freshly ground
pepper

2 cups (16 fl oz/500 ml) half-and-
half (half cream)

1½ cups (12 fl oz/375 ml) whole
milk

½ teaspoon nutmeg

roasted carrots with orange zest

1 package (2 lb/1 kg) baby carrots

1 package (10 oz/315 g) frozen pearl onions, thawed

4 tablespoons (2 oz/60 g) unsalted butter, at room temperature, cut into bits

1 tablespoon honey

1 tablespoon fresh thyme leaves

Zest of 1 orange, finely chopped

Coarse salt and freshly ground pepper

When roasted, carrots develop a caramelized sweetness without losing their crisp bite. (See photograph on page 105.)

Preheat the oven to 425°F (220°C). Place the carrots and onions on a baking sheet large enough to hold them in a single layer. Dot with the butter, drizzle with the honey, and sprinkle with the thyme and orange zest. Season with salt and pepper. Using your hands, toss the carrots and onions until evenly coated with the butter and seasonings. Spread the carrots and onions out into a single layer and roast for 15 minutes. Stir and continue to roast until the carrots and onions are golden brown and tender when pierced with a fork, 15–20 minutes longer. Transfer the roasted vegetables to a warmed serving bowl or platter and serve at once.

5 MINUTES PREPARATION

35 MINUTES COOKING

PREPARATION TIP
Use a vegetable peeler to remove the zest from the orange in wide strips, leaving the white pith behind, and then finely chop the strips with a chef's knife.

sautéed green beans with almonds and mustard butter

3 lb (1.5 kg) haricots verts or small Blue Lake green beans, trimmed

1 cup (4 oz/125 g) sliced (flaked) almonds

4 tablespoons (2 oz/60 g) unsalted butter

2 tablespoons coarse-grain mustard

Freshly ground pepper

To save time, you can parboil the green beans in advance and then quickly sauté them at the last minute.

Bring a large pot three-fourths full of lightly salted water to a boil. Add the green beans and boil until half-cooked, 3–4 minutes. Drain, refresh with cold water, drain again, and pat dry with paper towels. Set aside. (The beans can be prepared up to this point, covered, and refrigerated for up to 24 hours.)

In a large, dry frying pan over medium heat, toast the almonds, stirring constantly, until golden, about 3 minutes. Transfer to a plate and set aside. Return the pan to medium heat, melt the butter, and stir in the mustard. Add the green beans and sauté until heated through and starting to sear, about 5 minutes. Sprinkle in the almonds and toss until well combined. Season to taste with pepper, transfer to a warmed serving platter, and serve at once.

EACH RECIPE SERVES 12

5 MINUTES PREPARATION

15 MINUTES COOKING

PREPARATION TIP
Buy pretrimmed green beans to save prep time.

berry shortcake pudding with whipped cream

15 MINUTES
PREPARATION

PREPARATION TIP
Assemble the
pudding the evening
before to allow
the flavors to marry
and to help minimize
last-minute
preparations.

For variations, use chocolate or pistachio ice cream in place of vanilla, frozen cherries or peaches instead of the berries, and orange or lemon pound cake rather than plain.

Microwave the ice cream until just melted, about 1 minute on medium power. Alternatively, set the ice cream on the counter until melted, about 30 minutes. Set aside.

Using a food processor or blender, purée half of the berries until smooth. Pour the purée into a bowl and stir in the remaining berries.

Using half of the pound cake slices, line the bottom of a 9-by-13-inch (23-by-33-cm) baking dish. Drizzle half of the melted vanilla ice cream over the pound cake slices and then spoon half of the berry mixture over the ice cream and cake, spreading it in an even layer. Repeat the layers. Cover with plastic wrap and weight the top with a slightly smaller baking dish. Refrigerate for at least 4 hours or up to 24 hours, to allow the layers to compress.

Just before serving, in a large bowl, using an electric mixer on medium-high speed, whip the cream with the confectioners' sugar until soft peaks form, about 3 minutes.

To serve, remove the berry pudding from the refrigerator and remove the top baking dish and the plastic wrap. Cut the pudding into 12 equal servings. Top each serving with a dollop of whipped cream and a sprinkle of orange zest. Top with a few berries, if desired.

SERVES 12

1 pt (16 fl oz/500 ml) vanilla ice cream

2 packages (1 lb/500 g each) mixed frozen berries, thawed and drained

2 pound cakes, each 9 by 5 inches (23 by 13 cm), cut into slices $\frac{1}{2}$ inch (12 mm) thick

1 cup (8 fl oz/250 ml) heavy (double) cream

2 tablespoons confectioners' (icing) sugar

Grated orange zest for garnish

Mixed fresh berries for garnish (optional)

midweek dinner

tips and shopping notes

- Prepare the menu ahead of time and finish just before guests arrive.

- Set the table in the morning. Use place mats or a runner to dress it informally.

- Serve wine in all-purpose wineglasses and water in tumblers with clean lines.

- Pick up a freshly baked loaf of crusty bread on your way to or from work.

- For wine, serve a Syrah-Rhône blend or a Sangiovese for a red and a Riesling or Pinot Gris for a white.

menu

Campari and Orange Cocktails

•

Bresaola and Olives

•

*Baked Gnocchi with Taleggio,
Pancetta, and Sage*

•

Mâche and Escarole Salad with Crostini

•

Frozen Tiramisu

work plan

IN ADVANCE

Assemble the gnocchi

Assemble the tiramisu

Prepare the vinaigrette

JUST BEFORE SERVING

Mix the campari cocktails

Assemble the bresaola platter

Bake the gnocchi

Toss the salad

assemble several small, clear glass bottles with a variety of interesting shapes and textures, and fill them half full with water.

place a few poppy stems in each vase, keeping each arrangement light and delicate. Use a single color of bloom in each vase, or mix the colors.

arrange the bottles in a line running down the center of the table, taking care to place them so they will not block sight lines.

poppy vase centerpiece

Colorful poppies and assorted glass bottles make for an easy and striking centerpiece. If poppies are not available, use other unfussy long-stemmed flowers, such as Gerber daisies, zinnias, or dahlias.

campari and orange cocktails

5 MINUTES
PREPARATION

*Having a special cocktail ready to welcome your guests signals
the end of the workday and the start of a relaxed social evening.
A selection of savory nuts or chips is a good balance for the alcohol
and will stimulate the appetite for the meal to come.*

Put 4 old-fashioned glasses or other short, stocky glasses in the freezer to
chill for at least 15 minutes. Just before serving, fill a cocktail shaker half full
with crushed ice. Pour in the orange juice, Campari, Grand Marnier, and
vodka. Cover with the lid and shake vigorously for about 10 seconds. Pour
into the chilled glasses, dividing evenly. Garnish each glass with an orange
slice. Serve at once.

SERVES 4

Crushed Ice

1 cup (8 fl oz/250 ml) fresh
orange juice

1/4 cup (2 fl oz/60 ml) Campari

1/4 cup (2 fl oz/60 ml) Grand
Marnier or other orange liqueur

1/4 cup (2 fl oz/60 ml) vodka
or gin

4 orange slices

bresaola and olives

5 MINUTES
PREPARATION

*Put together a selection of olives from your favorite olive bar to offer
to guests as they sip their aperitifs before dinner. They go perfectly
with thin slices of* bresaola, *salty Italian-style air-cured beef.*

To serve, put the olives in a bowl and place the bowl on one end of a platter
or cutting board. Arrange the *bresaola* slices on the platter alongside the
bowl. Provide a small empty bowl or ramekin where guests can discard
the olive pits.

SERVES 4

1 container (8 oz/250 g) mixed
olives

1/2 lb (250 g) *bresaola*, prosciutto,
or spicy *coppa*, sliced paper-thin

baked gnocchi with taleggio, pancetta, and sage

2 tablespoons unsalted butter

2 packages (13 oz/410 g each) fresh gnocchi

$^1/_4$ lb (125 g) sliced pancetta, cut into $^1/_2$-inch (12-mm) pieces

2 tablespoons chopped fresh sage

$1^1/_2$ cups (12 fl oz/375 ml) half-and-half (half cream)

$^1/_2$ lb (250 g) Taleggio cheese, rind removed, cut into $^1/_4$-inch (6-mm) cubes

$^1/_4$ cup (1 oz/30 g) toasted bread crumbs

Freshly ground pepper

You can also make this recipe using 1 pound (500 g) tube-shaped dried pasta, such as penne. For a slightly less rich option, substitute fontina or Asiago cheese for the Taleggio.

Preheat the oven to 375°F (190°C). Butter four 7-inch (18-cm) shallow oval baking dishes.

Cook the gnocchi according to the package directions. Drain and set aside.

Lay the pancetta pieces in a single layer in a large cold frying pan. Place the pan over medium heat and cook until the pancetta starts to brown, about 2 minutes. Using a spatula, turn the pancetta pieces over and cook until browned, about 2 minutes longer. Remove from the heat and stir in the sage, gnocchi, half-and-half, and Taleggio.

Transfer the gnocchi mixture to the prepared baking dishes, dividing evenly. Sprinkle the tops with the bread crumbs and season with a few grinds of pepper. (The gnocchi can be prepared up to this point, cooled to room temperature, covered with plastic wrap, and refrigerated for up to 24 hours. Remove from the refrigerator 30 minutes before baking.)

Bake the gnocchi until golden, about 15 minutes. Serve hot, directly from the oven.

SERVES 4

15 MINUTES
PREPARATION

20 MINUTES
COOKING

SHOPPING TIP
Packages of ready-made and vacuum-packed gnocchi are sold in the fresh pasta section of most supermarkets.

mâche and escarole salad
with crostini

10 MINUTES
PREPARATION

PREPARATION TIP
If you prefer to make
your own crostini,
brush thin slices
of day-old baguette
lightly with extra-
virgin olive oil and
toast in a preheated
350°F (180°C) oven
until crisp and lightly
golden, about
15 minutes. Let cool
and store in an
airtight container for
up to 2 weeks.

*Mâche is sold prewashed and ready to use in sealed bags.
It does not keep well once harvested, so pay special attention to
the expiration date on the package.*

To make the vinaigrette, in a small bowl, whisk together the olive oil, lemon juice, and shallot. Season to taste with salt and pepper. (The vinaigrette can be prepared in advance, covered, and kept at room temperature for up to 4 hours.)

Remove the tough, fibrous exterior leaves from the escarole and discard. Tear the interior leaves into bite-sized pieces. Using a salad spinner, rinse and drain the escarole. Store in a zippered plastic bag in the refrigerator until ready to serve.

In a large bowl, combine the escarole and mâche. Whisk the vinaigrette, drizzle it over the greens, and toss to coat the leaves well. Arrange the crostini around the perimeter of the bowl. To serve, divide the salad greens among individual plates and accompany each serving with 2 crostini.

SERVES 4

LEMON-SHALLOT VINAIGRETTE

$1/4$ cup (2 fl oz/60 ml) extra-virgin olive oil

2 tablespoons fresh lemon juice

1 shallot, minced

Coarse salt and freshly ground pepper

1 head escarole (Batavian endive)

1 bag (10 oz/315 g) mâche lettuce

8 store-bought toasted baguette crostini or cheese crisps

frozen tiramisu

1 cup (8 fl oz/250 ml) vanilla
ice cream

$^{1}/_{2}$ cup (4 fl oz/125 ml) strong
coffee

2 tablespoons coffee liqueur

1 package (3 oz/90 g) ladyfingers,
broken up into large crumbs,
about 3 cups

Cocoa powder for dusting

Bittersweet chocolate shavings
for garnish

*Here, the popular coffee-and-cocoa-laced Italian dessert is made
with ice cream in place of mascarpone cheese, and assembled
in individual molds to simplify serving. Prepare the desserts the
night before your dinner, so that all you have to do is slip them
free, garnish, and serve.*

Microwave the ice cream until just melted, about 1 minute on medium power.
Alternatively, set the ice cream on the counter until soft, about 20 minutes.
Select four $^{3}/_{4}$-cup (6–fl oz/180-ml) custard molds or ramekins. Line each
mold with a sheet of plastic wrap, allowing a 2-inch (5-cm) overhang.

In a small bowl, combine the coffee and coffee liqueur.

Place $^{1}/_{4}$ cup ($^{1}/_{4}$ oz/7 g) of the ladyfinger crumbs in the bottom of each
prepared mold. Moisten the crumbs with 2 teaspoons of the coffee mixture.
Top with 2 tablespoons of the ice cream and spread the surface smooth.
Using a fine-mesh sieve, lightly dust the ice cream with cocoa powder. Repeat
the layers. Add a final layer of ladyfinger crumbs, gently pressing them into
the ice cream to form a flat surface. Drizzle the remaining coffee mixture over
the surface, dividing evenly. Fold the overhanging plastic wrap over the top,
covering completely. Place the molds in the freezer for at least 2 hours or up
to 24 hours.

When ready to serve, remove the molds from the freezer and let sit for
15 minutes at room temperature. Unwrap the plastic and invert each mold
onto an individual dessert plate. Pull on the edges of the plastic wrap to help
unmold each tiramisu, then peel off the plastic wrap. Dust the tops with
cocoa powder and sprinkle with some chocolate shavings. Serve at once.

SERVES 4

20 MINUTES
PREPARATION

2 HOURS
FREEZING

PREPARATION TIP
To make chocolate
shavings, use a
paper towel to hold
a 4-oz (125-g) block
of chocolate over
a plate with the
narrowest side facing
up. Gently pull a
vegetable peeler
over the surface
until you have about
1 tablespoon shavings
for each serving.

wine & cheese party

work plan

IN ADVANCE

Unwrap the cheeses

Make the almond and date spread

Prepare the vinaigrette

JUST BEFORE SERVING

Garnish the cheese board

Slice the *saucisson sec* and breads

Open the wines

Toss the salad

tips and shopping notes

- Visit a good cheese store several days ahead of time to get recommendations and to taste samples. Place your order a day ahead.

- Ask your wine merchant to suggest wine that will complement your cheese selections. Or, if you are rushed for time, choose a Malbec or Pinot Noir for a red and a Viognier or Sauvignon Blanc for a white.

- Set up the cheese board and the rest of the food on the sideboard, kitchen table, or island. Outfit the serving area with an assortment of antique knives, small plates, and napkins.

- Create a separate area for the wines, to keep traffic flowing smoothly.

- Write out the names of the cheeses and the wines being served on cards.

- For an easy dessert, serve coffee or *Vin Santo* with biscotti.

menu

Artisanal Cheese Board

•

Saucisson Sec

•

Roasted Almond and Date Spread

•

*Bibb Lettuce and Herb Salad
with Vinaigrette*

artisanal cheese board

To assemble an appealing cheese board, select a mix of types and textures—firm, semisoft, sheep's or goat's milk, double- or triple-crème, blue-veined —and serve alongside a selection of breads.

2 lb (1 kg) assorted cheeses (1/2–3/4 lb/250–375 g each of 3 or 4 cheeses), selecting from

> Firm cheeses: Cheddar, Gruyère, Comté, Manchego, Cantal, fontina, and Saint-Nectaire
>
> Semisoft cheeses: Muenster, Morbier, Bel Paese, Taleggio, and Vacherin
>
> Double- or triple-crème cheeses: Saint-André, Reblochon, Pont l'Évêque, Livarot, Camembert, Brie, and Boursault
>
> Blue-veined cheeses: Gorgonzola, Roquefort, Bleu de Bresse, Cabrales, and Fourme d'Ambert
>
> Goat's and sheep's milk cheeses: In the spring and summer, serve a fresh goat cheese; in the fall and winter, choose a medium-aged cheese such as Brebis Pyrénées, pecorino toscano, or Humboldt Fog

2 or 3 loaves bread, such as sourdough country loaf, a rustic walnut, and a baguette, sliced

Fresh grape or fig leaves for serving

Unwrap the individual cheeses and arrange them on a cheese board, marble slab, or large platter. Cover the arrangement with a large domed bowl and let stand at cool room temperature for 4–6 hours.

Just before serving, place grape leaves or fig leaves under each cheese. Put the breads on another board.

To store leftover cheese, wrap each piece in a sheet of waxed paper or parchment (baking) paper, place in individual zippered plastic bags, and store for up to 1 week in the refrigerator. To serve again, remove the cheeses from the plastic bags and protective paper. Arrange, cover with a bowl, and let come to room temperature.

SERVES 8

unwrap the selection of cheeses 4 to 6 hours ahead of time so they come to room temperature; select a large, sturdy cutting board, platter, or piece of marble or slate.

clip nontoxic leaves from the garden, such as fig, grape, citrus, olive, or apple leaves. Rinse the leaves well and put the cut ends in water until ready to use.

place the leaves on the cheese board just before serving, and put a cheese on each leaf. Keep the arrangement uncluttered and airy. Add cheese spreaders or knives for serving.

saucisson sec

5 MINUTES
PREPARATION

Saucisson sec is the term used for any French dry-cured salami-like sausage, though it is most commonly made from pork and is usually flavored with peppercorns, garlic, and herbs. Some types are coated with herbs or studded with pistachios or hazelnuts (filberts).

Using a sharp knife, cut the sausages into slices about ¼ inch (6 mm) thick and arrange on a plate. Set the plate alongside the cheeses and breads.

SERVES 8

2 *saucissons sec*, about
8 oz (220 g) each

roasted almond and date spread

5 MINUTES
PREPARATION

PREPARATION TIP
Make a double batch
of this spread and
freeze half of it. The
spread will keep for
up to 2 weeks.

When available, use pitted Medjool dates, which are meatier and sweeter than other varieties. Roasted pistachios or pecans can be used in place of the almonds. The spread is good on any of the breads suggested with the cheese board.

In a food processor, combine the almonds, dates, Madeira, and orange zest. Pulse until the almonds are finely ground and the mixture is almost smooth. (The spread can be prepared up to this point, transferred to a container, covered, and refrigerated for up to 1 week. Let the spread come to room temperature before serving.)

When ready to serve, transfer the spread to a small serving bowl. Set the bowl alongside the cheeses and breads.

SERVES 8

½ cup (2½ oz/75 g) unsalted
roasted whole almonds

1 package (8 oz/250 g)
pitted dates

¼ cup (2 fl oz/60 ml) Madeira or
dry sherry

Zest of 1 orange

bibb lettuce and herb salad with vinaigrette

Buy heads of "live" Bibb lettuce, hydroponically grown and shipped with roots still attached in plastic containers. If the roots are kept moist, the lettuces will remain garden fresh in the vegetable drawer of your refrigerator for up to a week. You can substitute arugula (rocket) or chicory, both peppery greens, for the lettuce.

To make the vinaigrette, in a small bowl, whisk together the olive oil, vinegar, garlic, and mustard. Season to taste with salt and pepper. Let stand at room temperature for at least 30 minutes or up to 4 hours, to allow the flavors to blend.

In a large serving bowl, combine the lettuce, chervil, tarragon, and parsley. Whisk the vinaigrette, drizzle it over the greens, and toss to coat the leaves well. Serve at once.

SERVES 8

VINAIGRETTE

6 tablespoons (3 fl oz/90 ml) olive oil

3 tablespoons red wine vinegar

1 clove garlic, pressed

1 teaspoon Dijon mustard

Coarse salt and freshly ground pepper

2 heads Bibb lettuce, leaves separated and torn into bite-sized pieces

1 bunch chervil, tough stems removed

1 bunch tarragon, tough stems removed

1 cup (1 oz/30 g) fresh flat-leaf (Italian) parsley leaves

10 MINUTES PREPARATION

STORAGE TIP
To keep herbs fresh, wrap them loosely in a damp paper towel and store in a zippered plastic bag in the vegetable drawer of the refrigerator.

INDEX

ACKNOWLEDGMENTS

WELDON OWEN wishes to thank the following individuals and organizations for their kind assistance: Desne Ahlers, Carrie Bradley, Ken DellaPenta, Sharon Silva, Steve Siegelman, Melissa Griggs, Tina and John Mehan, Dawn Low and John Owen, Tina-Lise and David Curtis, Jeff Dodge and his staff at La Farine, Lulu Rae Chocolates, Market Hall Produce, The Meadows, The Pasta Shop, and Vino.

GEORGE DOLESE would like to thank his associate, Elisabet der Nederlanden, for her contribution to the writing and styling of the recipes featured in this book. It was an honor to work so closely with such a beautiful person. Thank you "Betty"; Sue Conley and the Cowgirl Creamery for sharing their knowledge on cheese; Kuhn Rikon for making quality cookware; Anna Williams for making our food look so good on film and for her calming presence on set; Robin Turk for the beautiful table styling; Steve Siegelman for adding his writing talents to the text; Nicky Collings for her humor and artistic eye; Amy Marr for her sincere love of life; Hannah Rahill and the staff at Weldon Owen for being such a loyal client, and Chuck Williams for his appreciation of the simple things in life and his desire to share these things with the rest of the world.

ANNA WILLIAMS would like to thank her assistant on this project, Nick Wagner.

PHOTO CREDITS

ANNA WILLIAMS, alll photography, except for the following:

BILL BETTENCOURT: Pages 14–17, 18 (right), 19, 20–21, 24–25, 27–28, 31, 36–39, 40 (left), 41 (left), 45, 48–49, 61 (upper left)

FREE PRESS

A Division of Simon & Schuster, Inc.

1230 Avenue of the Americas

New York, NY 10020

A WELDON OWEN PRODUCTION

First printed in 2005

Printed in China

FREE PRESS and colophon are registered trademarks of
Simon & Schuster, Inc.

For information regarding special discounts for bulk
purchases, please contact Simon & Schuster Special Sales
at 1 800 456 6798 or business@simonandschuster.com

Printed by Midas Printing Limited

10 9 8 7 6 5 4 3 2 1

Library of Congress Cataloging-in-Publication Data is available.

ISBN-13: 978-0-7432-7852-2

ISBN-10: 0-7432-7852-6

Jacket Images

Front cover: Smoked Salmon with Garnishes, page 31.
Back cover: Bresaola and Olives, page 123; Poppy Vase Centerpiece, page 121;
Wine and Cheese Party, page 131.

THE ENTERTAINING SERIES

Conceived and produced by Weldon Owen Inc.

814 Montgomery Street, San Francisco, CA 94133

Telephone: 415-291-0100 Fax: 415-291-8841

In Collaboration with Williams-Sonoma, Inc.
3250 Van Ness Avenue, San Francisco, CA 94109

WILLIAMS-SONOMA, INC.
Founder & Vice-Chairman: Chuck Williams

WELDON OWEN INC.

Chief Executive Officer: John Owen

President and Chief Operating Officer: Terry Newell

Chief Financial Officer: Christine E. Munson

VP International Sales: Stuart Laurence

Creative Director: Gaye Allen

Publisher: Hannah Rahill

Associate Publisher: Amy Marr

Art Director: Nicky Collings

Design Consultant: Emma Boys

Designer: Rachel Lopez

Production Director: Chris Hemesath

Color Manager: Teri Bell

Production and Reprint Coordinator: Todd Rechner

Associate Food Stylist: Elisabet der Nederlanden

Photographer's Assistants: Nick Wagner, Heidi Ladendorf

Assistant Prop Stylists: Ginny Lau, Meghan Wood